I0831060

EYE VIEW BUGS AND OTHER TINY CREATURES

EYE VIEW BUGS AND OTHER TINY CREATURES

Catherine Ard

weldonowen

Contents

See the world in a whole new way!

Can you imagine what you might see if you were a fly zooming through the air or a shellfish scuttling along the seabed? We can never know *exactly* what animals see, but we can get a good idea from the amazing things scientists have discovered about their vision.

Different eyes work in different ways. Human eyes produce clear, colorful images. Not all animal eyes do that, but there are types of eyes that see faster, farther, or many more colors than we can. Once you know the science behind each creature's vision, you can take an imaginary look through their eyes. Prepare to be amazed!

Before you meet the bugs and other tiny creatures, let's explore some different types of eyes and discover how vision works.

The praying mantis uses its vision to track and trap its prey.

Simple eye

This eye consists of a cluster of **light-detecting cells** called **photoreceptors**. Simple eyes can tell if the world is **lighter or darker** and in **which direction**, but they **can't form images**. Animals with this type of eye include flatworms and starfish.

Starfish have a simple eye at the end of each of their five arms.

Pinhole eye

This **cup-shaped** eye can **form images**, but these are **quite dim** because of the **small amount of light** let in by the tiny hole at the front. Snails, giant clams, and abalones have this type of eye.

The giant clam's pinhole eyes see enough to tell it when there is danger approaching.

Compound eye

This eye is made up of hundreds or thousands of **cone-shaped sections** called **ommatidia**. Each ommatidium has a **lens** and **photoreceptor cells**. Many insects, including bees, flies, and beetles, have compound eyes.

Each of a dragonfly's ommatidium has a hexagonal surface called a facet.

Camera eye

This eye has a **lens** that focuses light onto the **retina**, which is like a screen packed with photoreceptors. This type of eye is found in birds, cephalopods, amphibians, reptiles, and mammals—including us! Human eyes have two types of photoreceptors—**cones and rods**.

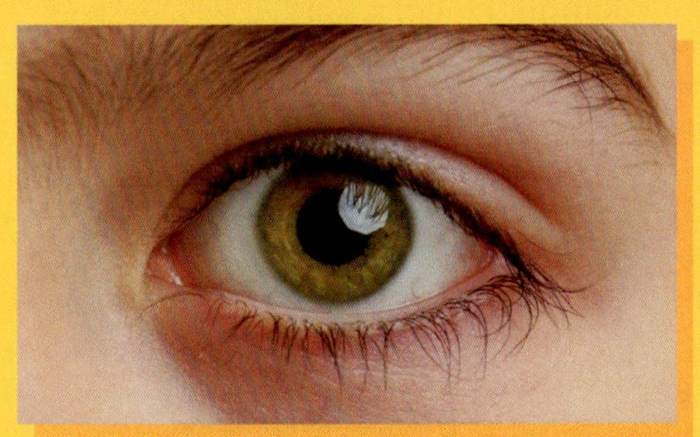

Human cone cells detect colors in bright light, while rod cells work in dim light to pick out the shapes of things.

What is light?

Eyes are designed to **detect light**. The light from the sun looks white, but it's actually made up of a rainbow of colors called a **spectrum**. The colors travel in **waves of different lengths**. The waves of light that humans can see are called "visible light." Some creatures, such as bees and mantis shrimp, can detect ultraviolet light and infrared light that are invisible to our eyes.

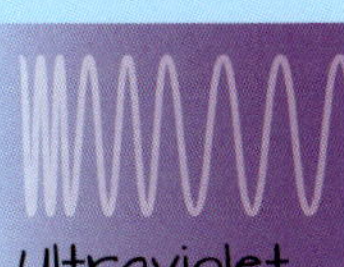

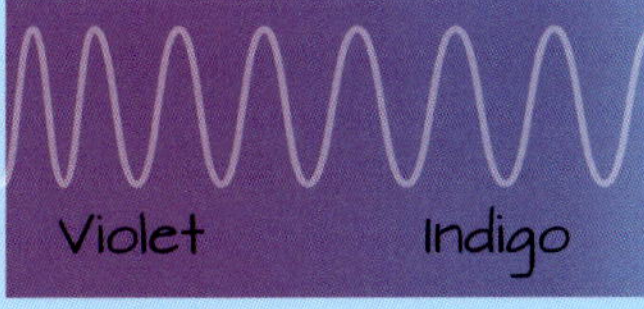

Color vision

Humans have **three types** of cone cells sensitive to red, blue, and green. By combining these colors, we can see about a million different shades. Some animals have **one**, **two, or four types** of photoreceptor. This means they see colors differently, or can only detect changes in brightness and see no colors at all.

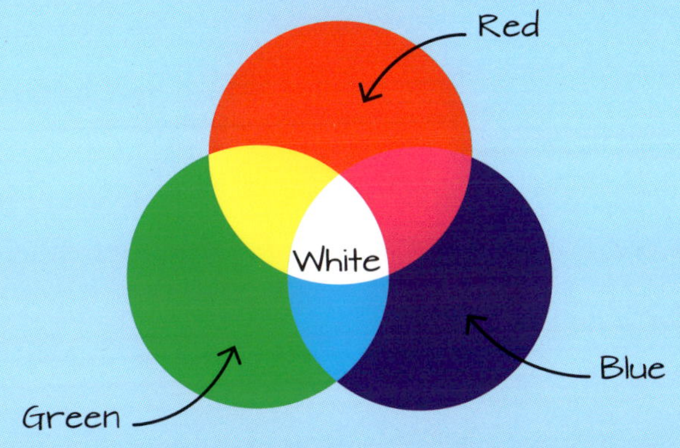

What you see

Everything that you can see without turning your head or moving your eyes is your **field of vision**. Your sharpest vision is in the **center** of your gaze where the view from both of your eyes is combined—this is your **binocular vision**. What you see above and below and on either side is fuzzier and less detailed. This is called **peripheral vision**. Animals have different fields of vision depending on the type and position of their eyes.

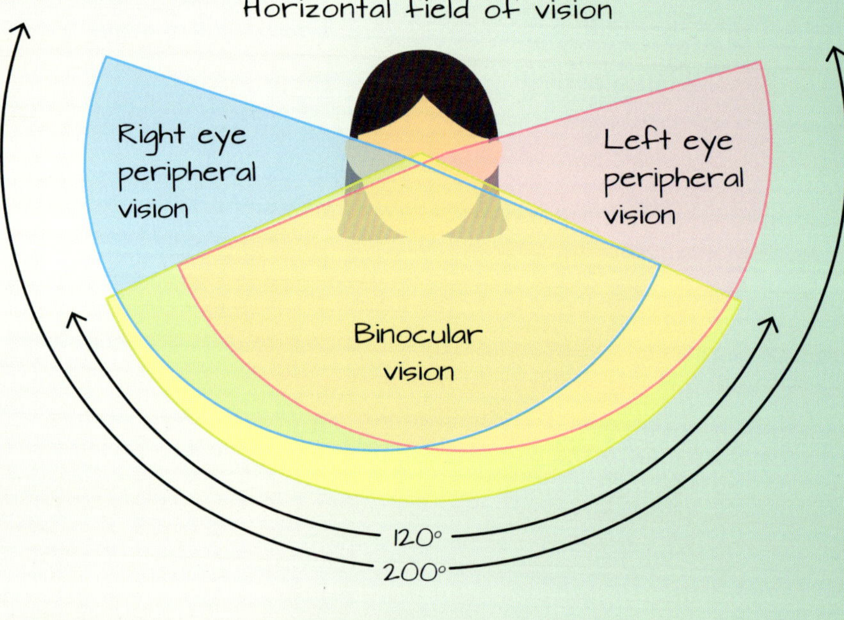

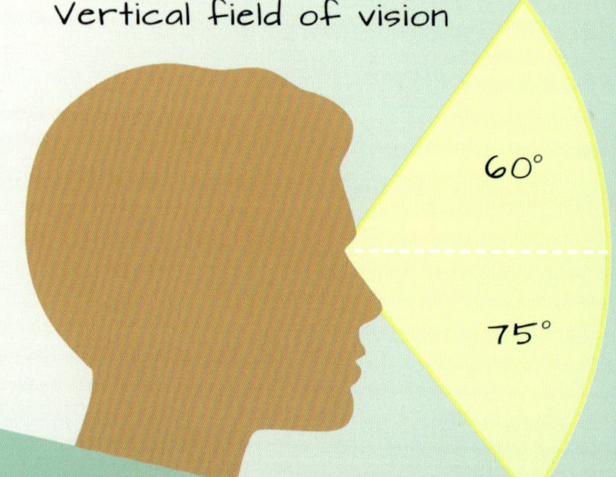

Seeing movement

Human eyes work by capturing up to **60 images per second**. When an object moves fast, our brain doesn't have time to process the information being sent by the eyes. That's why your hand **looks blurry** when you shake it in front of your face. Many bugs can see fast-moving objects much better than we can.

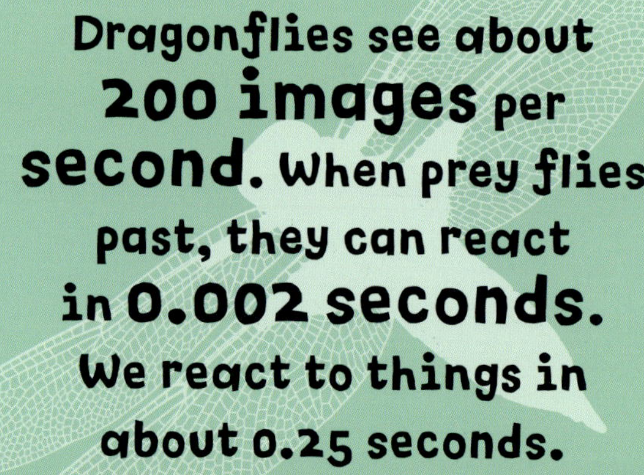

Dragonflies see about 200 images per second. When prey flies past, they can react in 0.002 seconds. We react to things in about 0.25 seconds.

All sorts of eyes

Over hundreds of millions of years, animals have evolved eyes that help them to **choose a mate, find food,** and **spot predators**. There are eyes built for **bright light in the day** or **darkness at night** and eyes that look in **opposite directions** at the same time. Some eyes are **lightning-fast** for tracking prey and others just see enough to **sense danger**.

Turn the page to discover some **awesome facts** about animal vision and **feast your eyes!**

Honey bee

This fuzzy insect's excellent eyes help it
Z-O-O-M in on flowers and
make a beeline back to the hive.

Busy buzzer

A honey bee's eyes are working overtime doing lots of different jobs. As well as spotting nectar-filled flowers, its eyes act like co-pilots, checking conditions so that the bee can fly efficiently and navigate back home. **The bee also has to keep an eye out for danger so that it can buzz to safety.**

Bees use the **Sun** to find their way around. They also have a way of knowing where the Sun is, even in **thick cloud.**

Eye View Checklist

- See in the dark
- See underwater
- See in very bright light ✔
- See all around them ✔
- Focus on something in the distance
- Focus on something up close ✔
- Good at detecting movement ✔

Large colonies of honey bees live together in hives, where they make honey and beeswax. Bees are also important pollinators.

Pixel-packed

Like most insects, honey bees have **two types of eyes**. Three small, **simple eyes** called **ocelli** sense light and movement. Two large, **compound eyes** detect color, brightness, shape, and movement. These give the bee a **pixelated** view of the world.

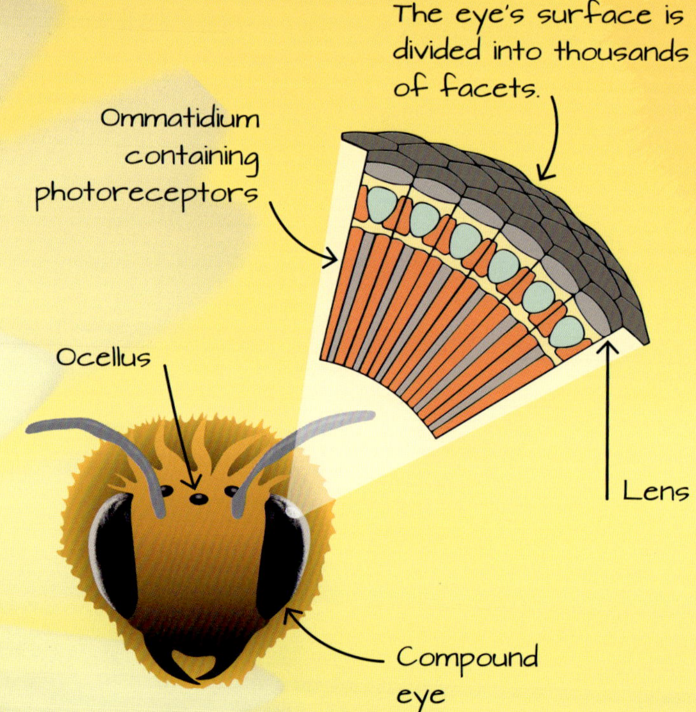

Hairy eyes

Some honey bees have **hairs that grow between the facets** of their compound eyes. These hairs detect the **wind's speed and direction**, helping the bee to adjust its flight so that it can do things like **hover** and **find its way back** to the hive. The hairs also act like eyelashes, **trapping pollen** that can fertilize the next flower the honey bee visits.

Ultra-vision

Bees can't see all the colors we can, but they can see a part of the light spectrum that humans can't see at all—**ultraviolet light**. Dark lines of ultraviolet on a flower's petals **guide bees to the nectar** at the center of the flower. We need a flower to be under a special ultraviolet light in order to see this.

Normal light

Ultraviolet light

Humans can see, on average, 30–60 separate images per second before they blur together. Honey bees can see 300!

Now turn the page for an imaginary view of what the honey bee sees when it's searching for nectar . . .

Our eye view

The honey bee has found its favorite flower . . .

With its sights set on reaching the nectar, will it spot a cunning and deadly predator on the flower petals?

Because we can't see ultraviolet light, we are unaware of the flower's guides to the nectar.

A honey bee's eye view!

Jumping spider

This pea-sized spider needs all of its
eight eyes to survive. It has to pinpoint
prey as well as hungry predators!

Mini marvel

This little leaper has the sharpest vision of any spider. Excellent eyesight helps the jumping spider to choose a mate, pick out dinner, and spot predators. **Whether it locks friends, enemies, or food in its steady gaze, it's always ready to spring into action!**

Eye View Checklist

- See in the dark
- See underwater
- See in very bright light ✔
- See all around them ✔
- Focus on something in the distance
- Focus on something up close ✔
- Good at detecting movement ✔

Jumping spiders are tiny. Some are smaller than a sesame seed.

Jumping spiders are only a few millimeters long, but they can leap more than 20 times their own body length.

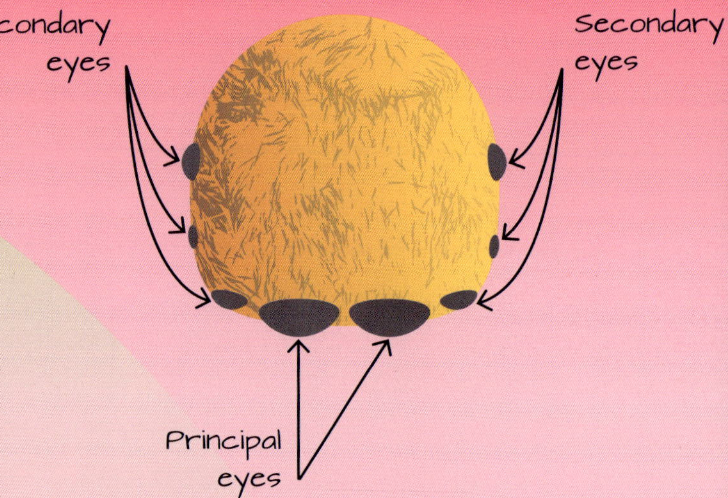

Multi-eyed

The jumping spider has **eight eyes** positioned around its head. Its two principal eyes can move and give it **sharp color vision**. The secondary eyes are fixed. They detect movement at the sides and from behind, but the image they produce is **gray and blurry**.

To attract a female, the male waves his legs around in a kind of dance. If she's impressed by his moves, she'll choose him for a mate.

X marks the spot

Using all its eyes together, the jumping spider has a field of vision of nearly **360 degrees**. The **principal eyes** give a detailed color image inside an **X-shape** and move to keep a predator or prey within that zone. The **front-facing secondary eyes** help the spider to **judge distance**.

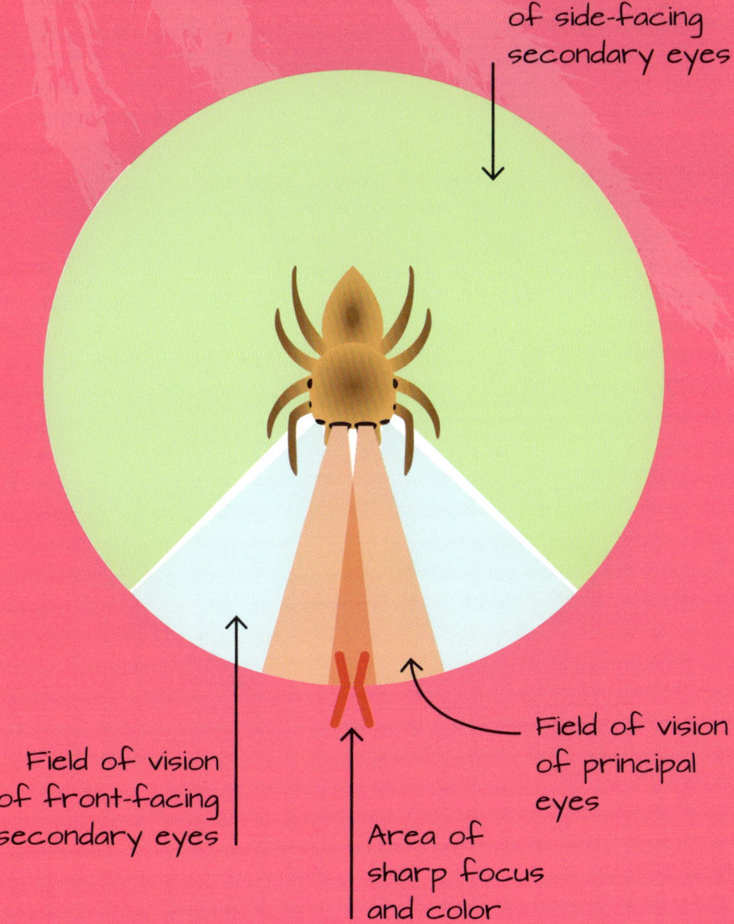

See like a spider

First, look straight ahead and waggle your thumbs at the sides of your head. This is your **peripheral vision**—what the spider sees with its secondary eyes. Now bring your fists together. The shape you make with your thumbs up is like the area the spider sees with its **sharpest vision**.

Now turn the page for an imaginary view of how the spider spots an approaching predator . . .

Our eye view

We can see less of the scene, but everything is in color and in focus.

A jumping spider is on high alert . . .

Toxic milkweed bugs are the least of its worries. The greater danger is the mud-dauber wasp—a fearsome predator!

Most spiders can't see red. The jumping spider can only identify the red milkweed bugs if it uses its principal eyes. It has learned to leave the nasty-tasting bugs alone.

A jumping spider's eye view!

Purple sea urchin

The purple sea urchin might look like a **pincushion**, but it's really a spine-covered sea creature. As it slowly moves around the seabed, it is **watching you** with **its feet!**

Prickly creature

A sea urchin doesn't have eyes, but if you get too close, it will point its sharp spines at you. So how does it know you're there? The wavy, tentacle-like tube feet poking out between the spines are the urchin's vision super-tool. **The urchin is an eyeless animal that sees with its feet!**

Eye View Checklist

- See in the dark
- See underwater ✔
- See in very bright light ✔
- See all around them ✔
- Focus on something in the distance
- Focus on something up close
- Good at detecting movement

Purple sea urchins can live as long as 70 years!

Handy feet

The urchin's test, or hard shell, is covered in holes. Poking out from these holes are **flexible tube feet**. A **tiny suction cup** on the end of each foot allows the urchin to **stick to surfaces** and pull itself around. Tube feet can be used for **cleaning spines** and **grabbing food** and passing it down to the mouth. Amazingly, these bendy survival tools are also **used for seeing**!

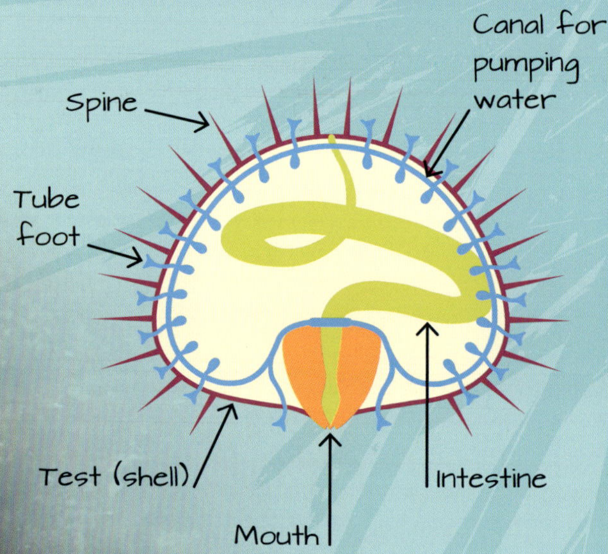

A purple sea urchin moves around using its tube feet. It extends or draws back its feet by pumping water in and out of them.

Footivision

The sea urchin's tube feet have **light-sensitive cells** at their base. When first one foot, then another senses a **change from light to dark**, speedy messages are sent along the nerves in the feet to tell the urchin that something is there. An urchin's **vision is not very clear** or detailed compared with human eyesight, but it is enough to help it seek shelter, find food, and hide from predators.

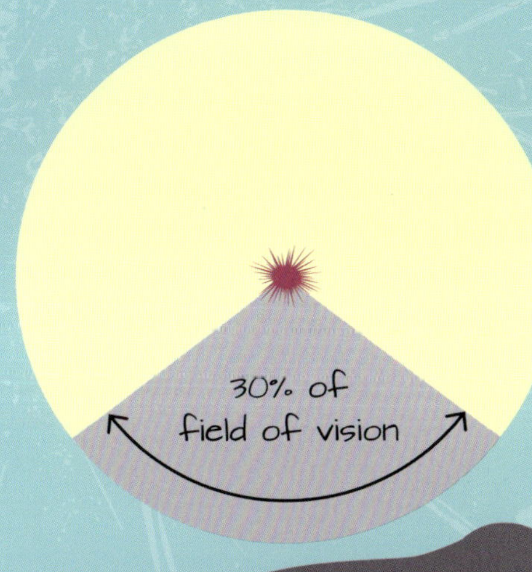

An object needs to fill 30–70 percent of the urchin's 360° field of vision before it can be detected.

Spiky snack

Purple sea urchins live in **large groups** called colonies and they **eat the kelp** that grows off the North American Pacific coast. Munching through the stalks of this long, wavy seaweed makes it drift away and die. Luckily, **sea otters** love eating prickly purple urchins. By **reducing the numbers** of urchins, they help protect the precious kelp forests.

Prickly sea urchins are echinoderms. This name comes from the ancient Greek term for "hedgehog skin."

Now turn the page for an imaginary view of what the purple sea urchin sees in the kelp forest . . .

Our eye view

A purple sea urchin joins its pals to gobble sea kelp . . .

The urchin's tube feet can detect a dark shape moving in the water. Is it a wavy strand of seaweed or something scarier?

A purple sea urchin's eye view!

With tube feet positioned all around its body, the urchin has a 360° view of its surroundings, including some nearby rocks.

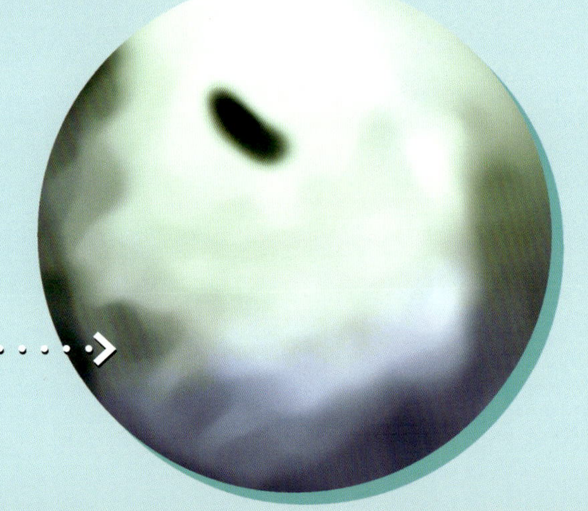

A shadow starts to fall on some of the feet, but it's not big enough for the urchin to detect anything.

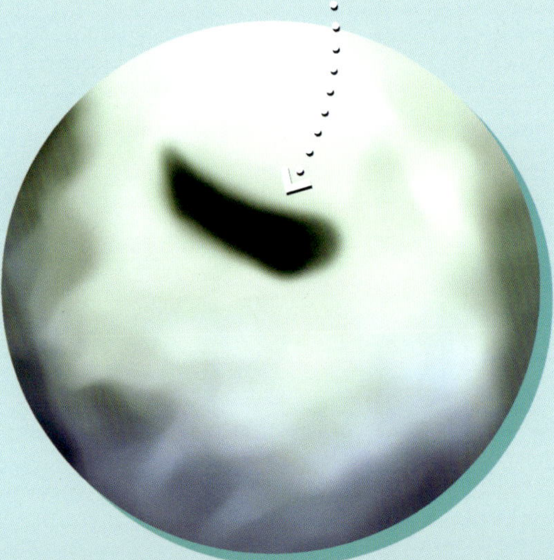

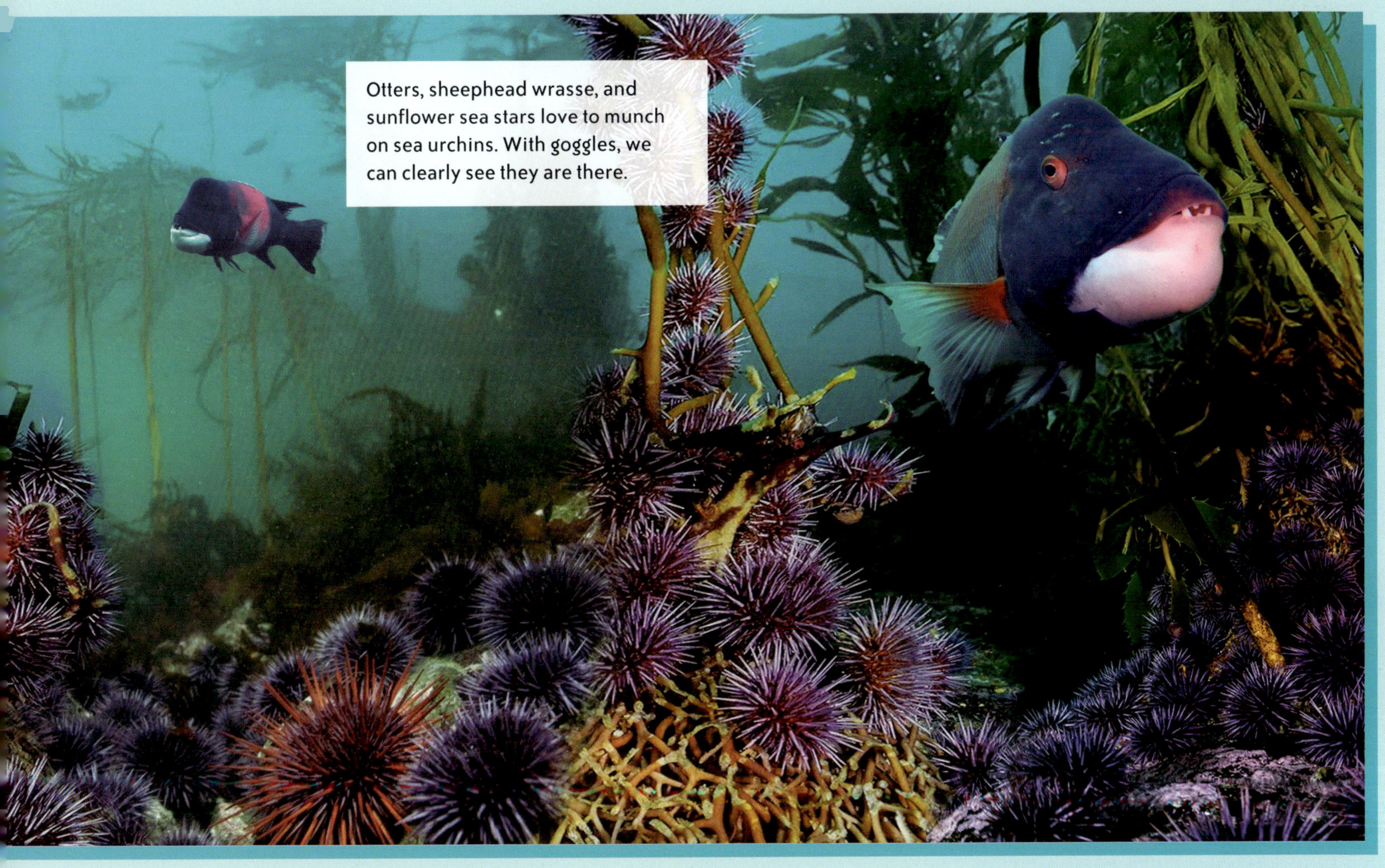

Otters, sheephead wrasse, and sunflower sea stars love to munch on sea urchins. With goggles, we can clearly see they are there.

As the object gets closer, it casts a shadow over more of the urchin's feet. Danger alert!

It's very close now—time to move to safety!

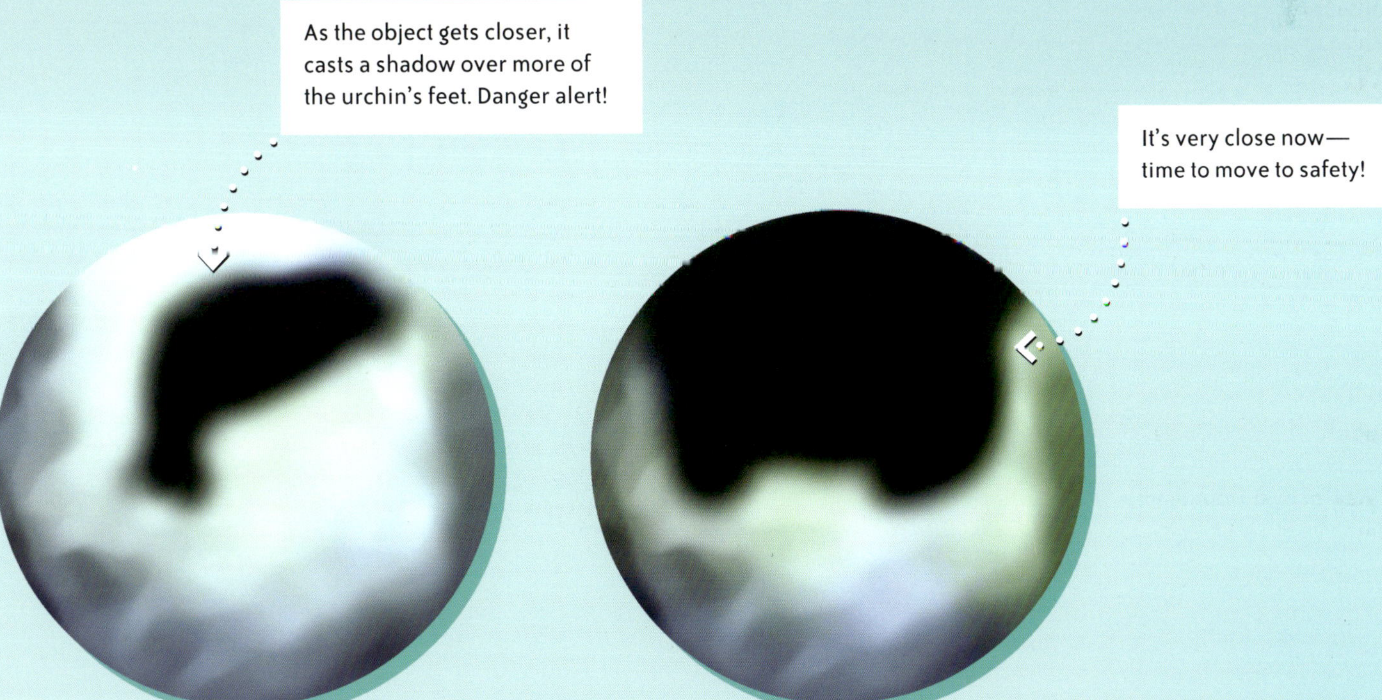

Dragonfly

Meet one of nature's **most deadly** aerial assassins! Guided by its **enormous eyes**, a dragonfly locks fast-moving insects in its sights, then **swoops in for the attack.**

Big-eyed flier

Like an old-fashioned airplane, the drone of a dragonfly's wings can be heard loud and clear as it patrols the water above a pond. This fast, ferocious predator has a slim, streamlined body, strong wings, powerful jaws, and eyes that wrap around its head like a jet pilot's helmet. **It's a lean, mean flying machine!**

Eye View Checklist

- See in the dark
- See underwater
- See in very bright light ✔
- See all around them ✔
- Focus on something in the distance ✔
- Focus on something up close
- Good at detecting movement ✔

Dragonflies have large compound eyes that meet at the top of their head. Their dazzling colors catch the light as they zoom around.

Thanks to its huge, curved eyes, a dragonfly can still see you after it has flown past.

Eyes in the sky

Dragonflies rely on their sight to hunt. Their eyes are highly sensitive to movement, giving them **lightning-fast reactions**. They can spot prey from the far side of a pond and pinpoint a single bug in a swarm. Dragonflies **attack in mid-air** from below and behind. As they **track an insect**, they angle their head to use the **sharpest part of their vision**—an area on the retina called the **fovea**, which is packed with photoreceptors.

The dragonfly can predict where to intercept the fly.

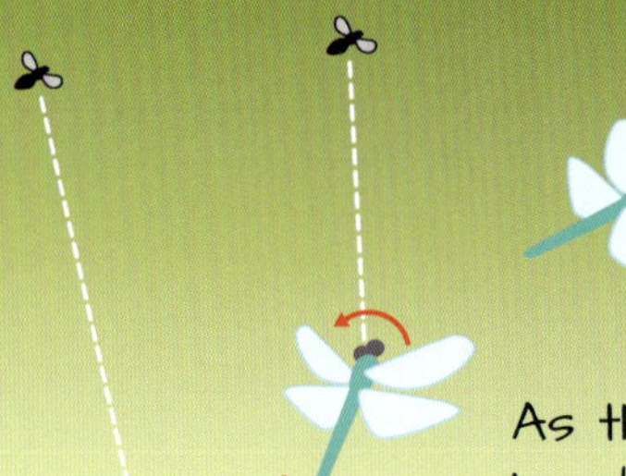

As the body turns, the head counter-rotates to target the fly using the fovea.

The dragonfly spots its prey and takes off.

Keeping level

With all its **zooming and looping**, it would be easy for the dragonfly to become totally disorientated—a bit like how you feel after you've spun around a few times. Luckily, its three **simple eyes**, called **ocelli**, are there to guide it. Ocelli help the dragonfly to know **which way is up** and keep its **flight stable** and **gaze level**.

Dragonfy ocelli are specially adapted to see a wide horizon.

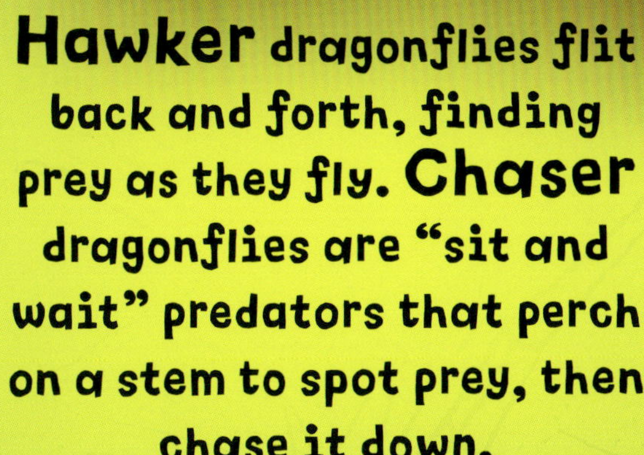

Hawker dragonflies flit back and forth, finding prey as they fly. Chaser dragonflies are "sit and wait" predators that perch on a stem to spot prey, then chase it down.

Transformers

A dragonfly spends most of its life underwater as a larva called a **nymph** or **naiad**. During this time, its compound eyes are **tuned specifically** to its murky, underwater world. After a few years, a nymph transforms into an adult and completely rebuilds a much bigger eye, with **enhanced color vision** that is perfect for high flying.

Now turn the page for an imaginary view of what the dragonfly sees when it's hunting by a pond . . .

Our eye view

We see much less of our surroundings than a dragonfly can.

A dragonfly darts across the water, its big eyes taking in everything as it goes . . .

The pond is busy with other dragonflies hunting for bugs. Luckily, there are plenty of insects to go around—and a few unwelcome visitors, too!

Both close things and faraway things are in focus at the same time.

The dragonfly's wraparound compound eyes form a 360° image made of tiny hexagons.

A dragonfly's eye view!

Peacock mantis shrimp

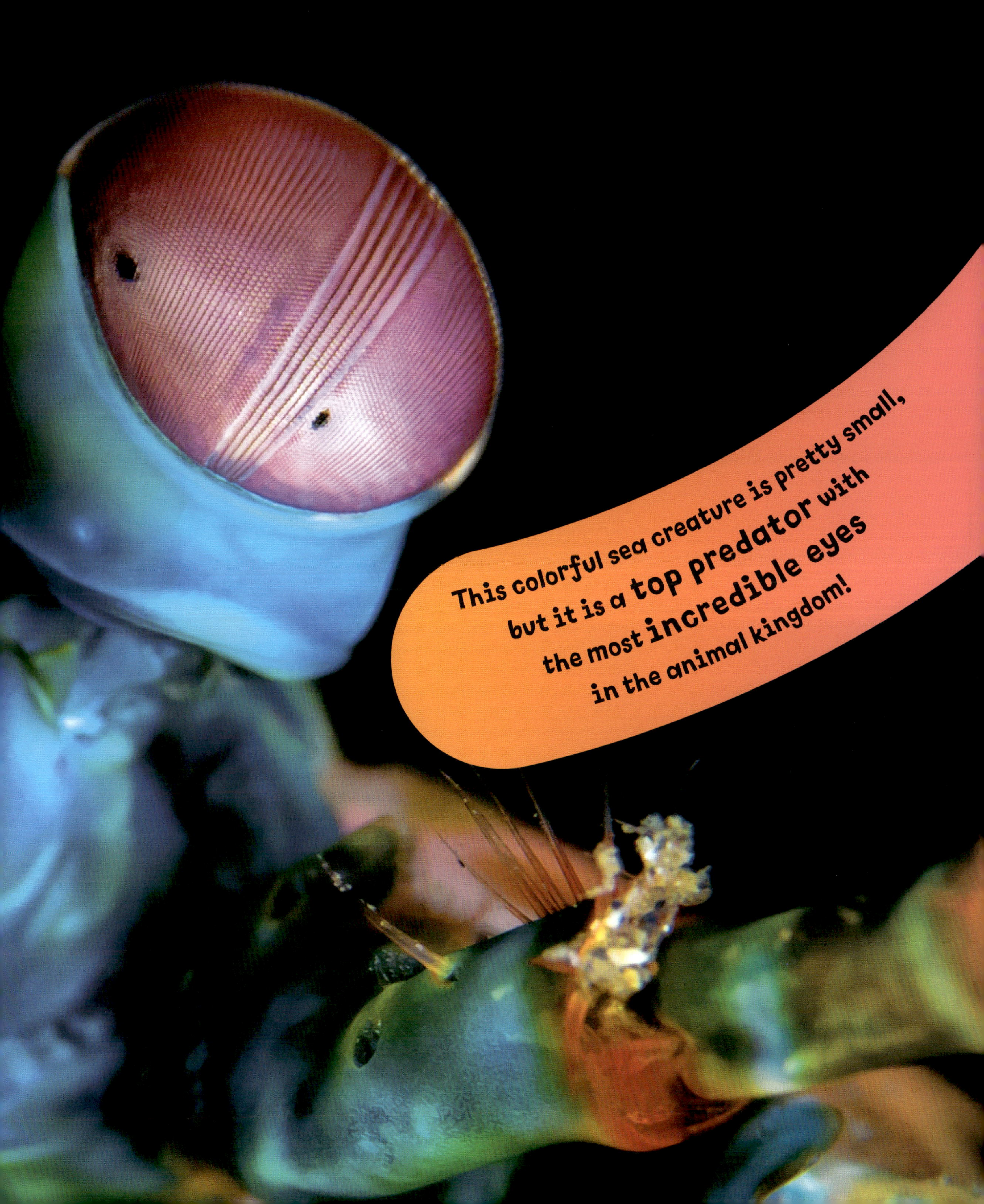
This colorful sea creature is pretty small,
but it is a top predator with
the most incredible eyes
in the animal kingdom!

Colorful killer

A peacock mantis shrimp as small as your hand scuttles along the seabed of the coral reef. Don't be fooled by its pretty rainbow-colored shell—this mini meat-eater batters its prey with its club-shaped front claws. To help it spot its victim, its extraordinary eyes can move separately from each other, rotate through almost 360 degrees, and look in different directions at the same time. **Watch out! This crustacean has super-powered eyes—and a powerful punch!**

Eye View Checklist

- See in the dark
- See underwater ✔
- See in very bright light ✔
- See all around them ✔
- Focus on something in the distance
- Focus on something up close ✔
- Good at detecting movement ✔

The peacock mantis shrimp isn't actually a shrimp. It's a stomatopod, a type of sea creature related to crabs and lobsters. It has existed since before the dinosaurs.

What a view!

The peacock mantis shrimp's vision is different from every other animal on the planet! Each eye is divided into **three bands**. The top and bottom bands allow the shrimp to see the **location, distance, and shape** of the objects around it. The middle band can **see colors** but **can't form images**.

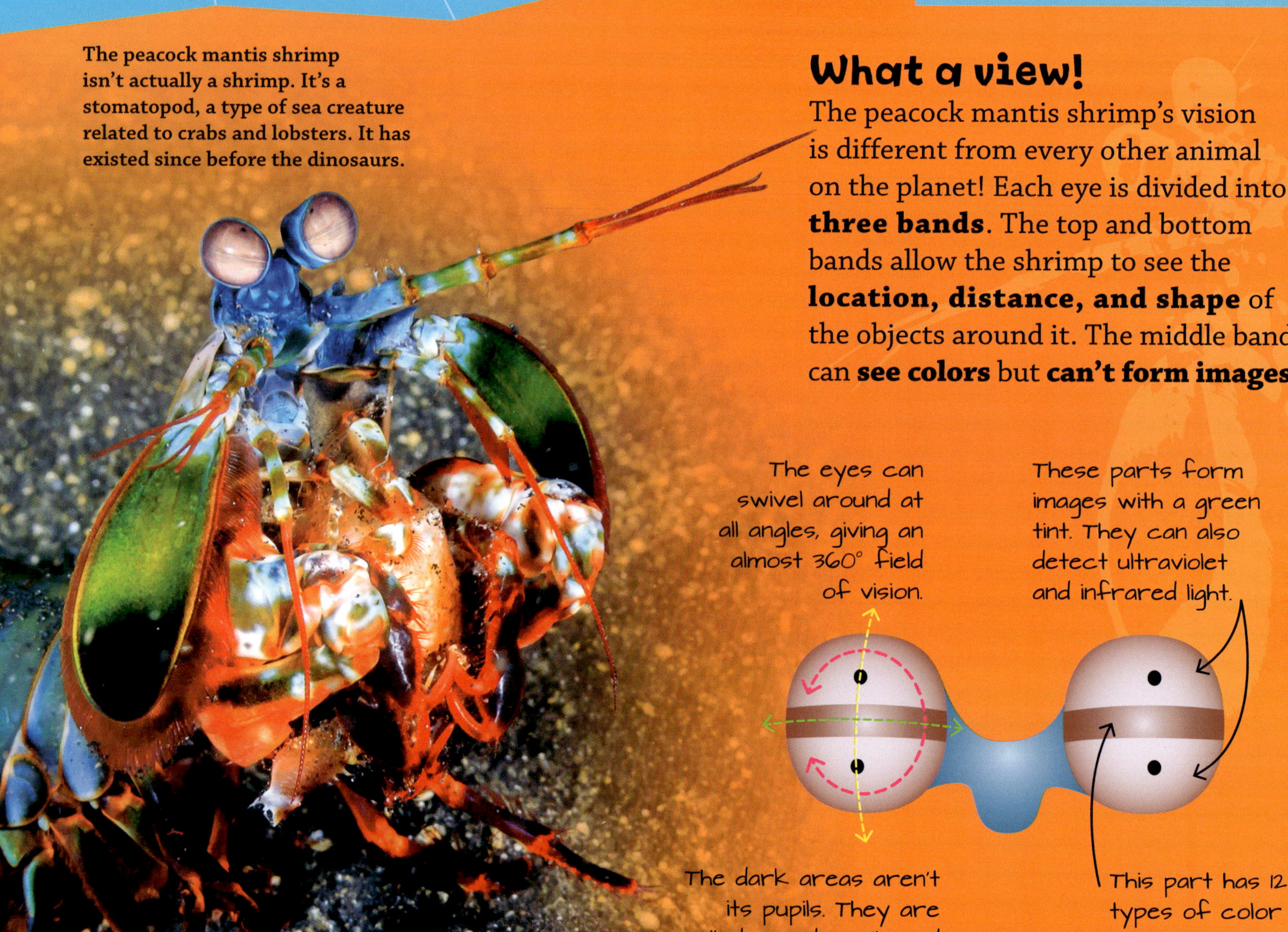

The peacock mantis shrimp has the **quickest** underwater **punch** of any known animal—so fast that it makes the **water boil!**

Super scanner

Scientists have discovered that the **middle parts** of the mantis shrimp's eye act like a **barcode scanner** at the supermarket. Although they **don't see images**, they take in basic **information about color** that allows the shrimp to **quickly recognize an object** as food, a threat, or a place of safety.

Smash and grab

To capture and eat crabs, snails, and clams, the peacock mantis shrimp **punches them** with the force of a flying bullet to smash through their shells. Humans need **both eyes**—binocular vision—to accurately judge the distance of an object. The shrimp can do it in **three ways** with **just one eye**. That makes it a terrific target-finder and punch-thrower!

Now turn the page for an imaginary view of the peacock mantis shrimp's colorful underwater world . . .

Our eye view

When we use swimming goggles, we can see colors and details clearly.

A peacock mantis shrimp can see all the comings and goings of the coral reef from its burrow . . .

An unsuspecting hermit crab will make a tasty snack, but there are dangers lurking, too. The mantis shrimp needs to keep scanning its surroundings or it could end up being lunch!

Mantis shrimp often flash their bright colors at potential mates to attract them or at rivals to scare them.

Peacock mantis shrimp can move their eyes in opposite directions, so they have a wide view of their surroundings.

A peacock mantis shrimp's eye view!

With the upper and lower parts of its eyes, the mantis shrimp sees in shades of green.

The large shape of a cuttlefish is easy to spot. The shrimp needs to hide in its burrow to avoid this predator.

The blue-ringed octopus would love a mantis shrimp for a meal.

Using all six of its eye bands, the shrimp can really focus in on its hermit crab prey.

Praying mantis

This big-eyed creature is not an alien from outer space.
It's an awesome insect predator—and it could be
hunting down dinner in a park or garden near you!

Praying predator

This mantis gets its name because it holds its front legs as if it's praying. In fact, it's just waiting for a juicy meal to pass by. Within a split second of spotting an insect, the mantis pins it down using the sharp spines on its front legs. Then it bites off its victim's head. Chomp! **The mantis uses its amazing binocular vision to pinpoint the exact distance of its prey.**

Looks that kill

A praying mantis is the only insect that can **turn its head 180 degrees** in either direction—that's way more than you looking over your shoulder. This means it can **scan its surroundings** while the rest of its body stays perfectly still, allowing it to surprise its prey. Each of the mantis's **large compound eyes** has up to 10,000 light-gathering ommatidia that help it to sense the tiniest of movements.

Eye View Checklist

- See in the dark
- See underwater
- See in very bright light ✔
- See all around them ✔
- Focus on something in the distance
- Focus on something up close
- Good at detecting movement ✔

The praying mantis has eyes on the corners of its triangular head for an all-around view. It blends in perfectly with green plants and even has markings on its wings to make them look like leaves.

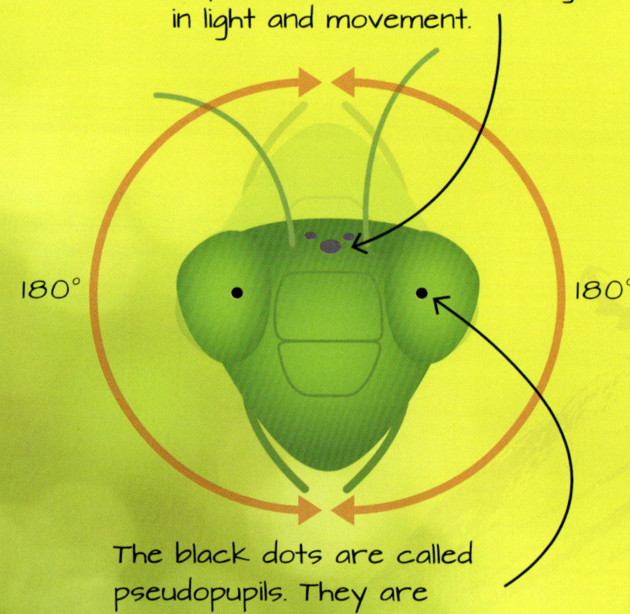

Mantises have a single ear on their belly that picks up the sounds made by bats. It alerts the insect to approaching danger.

Deadly double

The awesome praying mantis has a vision superpower. It is the only insect we know of that can **perceive depth** like we do, using both eyes at once. Its **brain combines the view from each eye** to form a single image—this is called stereopsis. This allows the mantis to **judge distances** accurately, so it can strike as soon as prey comes within reach.

Using both eyes, the mantis can judge whether prey is near or far away.

False eyes

The praying mantis is a top predator, feasting on grasshoppers, beetles, and bees, but it is also **prey to other animals**. Birds, bats, lizards, frogs, and large spiders can all make a meal of a mantis. When threatened, the mantis makes itself appear big and scary by spreading its wings and revealing **two fake eye spots** on its front legs. This usually frightens predators off!

Now turn the page for an imaginary view of what the praying mantis sees when it's waiting to pounce . . .

Our eye view

Crickets chirp and bees hum, but there is a cleverly disguised killer lurking in this sunny scene . . .

A praying mantis is ready to ambush its next victim—but there are other hungry hunters in the garden today.

A praying mantis's eye view!

Dung beetle

This humble little insect might spend its life **digging, pushing, and gobbling poop**, but it has **special eyes** to help it with some tricky tasks.

Busy bug

Dung beetles clean up the poop that grazing animals drop. They need it for food or as a place to lay their eggs. Some species tunnel under it, some live in mounds of it, and others pat it into balls and roll it away. Dung-rolling beetles are weightlifters and acrobats—and astro-navigators! **Their amazing eyes help them to use the sky to find their way around.**

Speedy takeout

Hundreds of dung beetles can descend on a pile of fresh poop. With **so much competition**, dung-rollers need to move their balls as **quickly** and as **far away** as possible if they want to keep hold of their stinky prize. To do this, they put their **heads down** and their **bottoms up** and use their strong back legs to push the ball along.

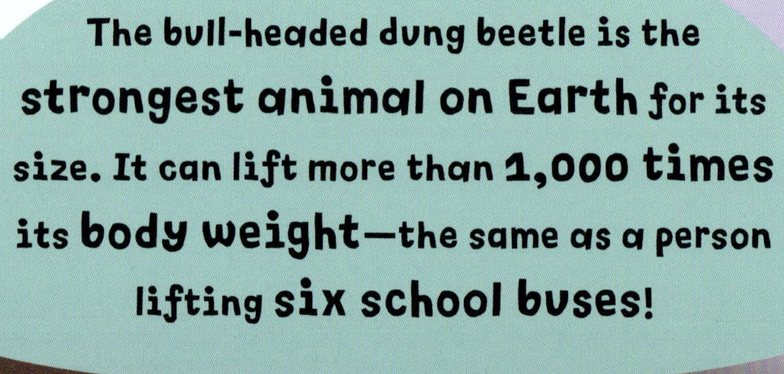

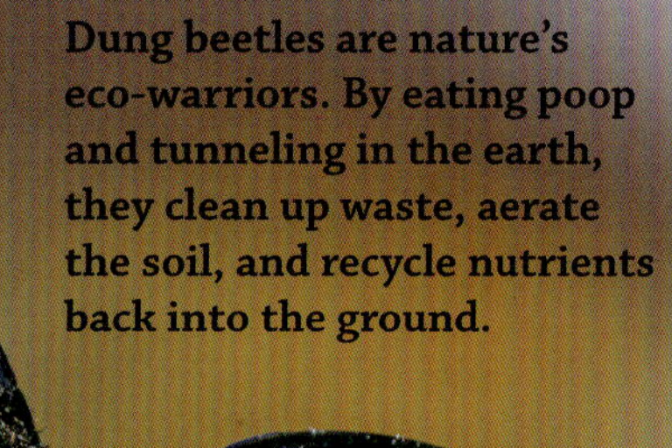
Dung beetles are nature's eco-warriors. By eating poop and tunneling in the earth, they clean up waste, aerate the soil, and recycle nutrients back into the ground.

Eye View Checklist

- See in the dark ✔
- See underwater
- See in very bright light ✔
- See all around them
- Focus on something in the distance ✔
- Focus on something up close
- Good at detecting movement

Dung-rollers can push their balls up to 650 feet—the length of two soccer fields!

Four-eyes

The dung beetle has a special type of eye to help with its astro-navigation. Like almost all insects, beetles have compound eyes, but a dung beetle's eyes are divided into **upper and lower parts**. The lower part **faces the ground** and helps it when it's flying. The upper part **faces the sky** and gives the beetle a good view of everything above it.

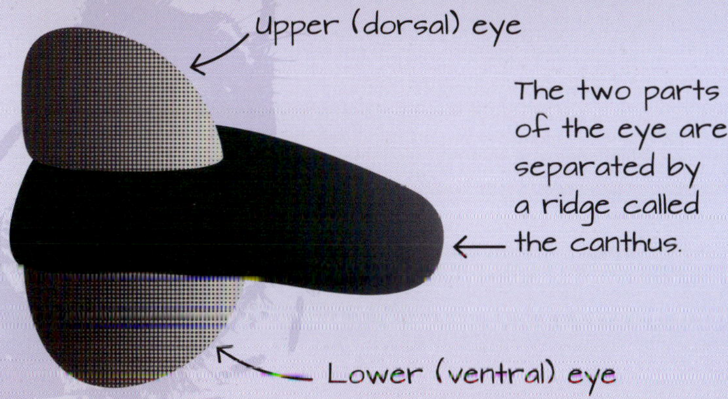

Dung beetle eye

Cosmic compass

The fastest route to roll away a dung ball is in a **straight line**, but keeping to this when you're walking backward is tricky! To stay on track, dung beetles **fix their sights** on one point. Daytime dung beetles use the **Sun's position** as a guide. Nocturnal beetles navigate using the **Moon or the stars**. Their eyes are not sensitive enough to see single spots of light, but they can see the **Milky Way**.

Dung, or animal poop, contains tasty bits of undigested food that dung beetles and their larvae can feast on. Yum yum!

Now turn the page for an imaginary view of what the dung beetle sees when it's rolling away a ball of dung . . .

Our eye view

A herd of African elephants has just dumped piles of poop, and the dung beetles have moved in . . .

One beetle starts to roll its dung ball away to safety, but it needs to watch out for thieving rivals and hungry predators!

A dung beetle's eye view!

Strawberry conch

These comical googly eyes
belong to a shy little sea snail.
It peers out from under its shell to make sure
the coast is clear of hungry predators!

Super snooper

The strawberry conch is named for its rosy, strawberry-sized shell. It lives around tropical shores, chomping on the algae that grows on coral and sandy seabeds. Most slugs and snails have tiny eyes and very bad sight, but this beady-eyed sea snail is different. **Its excellent eyes act like periscopes!**

Eye View Checklist

- See in the dark
- See underwater ✔
- See in very bright light ✔
- See all around them
- Focus on something in the distance
- Focus on something up close ✔
- Good at detecting movement ✔

The strawberry conch has eyes ten times bigger than those of land snails. Despite being beautifully colored themselves, the eyes can't see colors at all.

Take a peek

Conches have a **wide field of vision** because their eyes are located at the end of **flexible stalks** that swivel and bend. Each eye can **move independently** in different directions, so the conch gets a good view of its surroundings. The eye stalks are also retractable, which means the conch can not only **extend them** to look around but **pull them back** inside its shell if it detects danger.

Champion eyes

There is no contest when it comes to the best snail vision—the strawberry conch is the clear winner. A land snail has **pinhole eyes** that can only see **blurry patches** of light and dark. The strawberry conch sea snail has **large, camera-type eyes**, much the same as ours. These have a lens to focus light and a retina packed with almost **100,000 photoreceptors**, which give detailed vision.

If a strawberry conch loses an **eye**, it can **grow a new one** just as good as the one it lost!

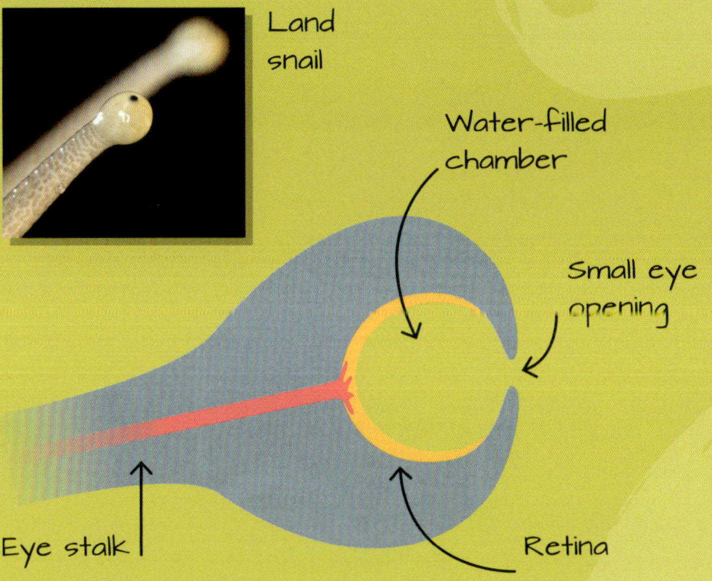

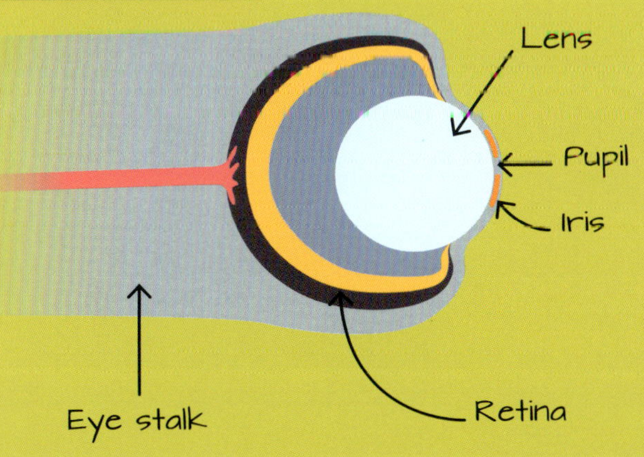

Look and leap

As well as sharp eyes, the conch has **sensory tentacles** at the base of its eyestalks, which **detect chemicals** in the surrounding water. This helps it to find food—and avoid predators! If it needs to make a speedy escape, the strawberry conch doesn't slide away like a land snail. Instead, it **leaps to safety** by pushing off the seabed with its claw-shaped "foot."

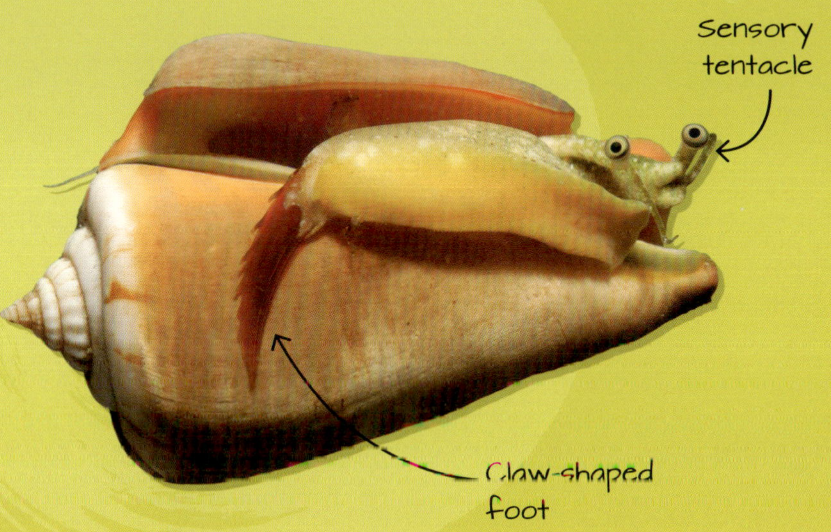

Now turn the page for an imaginary view of what the strawberry conch sees on the seabed . . .

Our eye view

Using goggles, we see a colorful underwater scene packed with coral, fish, and shellfish.

The conch can spot small objects, like the venomous cone snail. Using its springy foot, it can leap away from this slow mover.

Strawberry conches can't see colors, but they can see more of their surroundings and lots of detail.

A strawberry conch cautiously peeks out of its shell and looks around . . .

Other conches are feeding on the green algae, but what's that shape looming in the distance? It could be time to take SHELL-ter . . . or leap to safety!

A strawberry conch's eye view!

Hummingbird
hawk-moth

This hairy little creature looks
more like a bird than an insect.
Listen for the hum of its fast-beating wings
as it uses precision vision
to suck up delicious nectar from flowers.

Hairy hoverer

The hummingbird hawk-moth looks and behaves so much like a hummingbird that it was named after it. Just like the bird, this little creature flies during the day—most other moths come out at night. You'll spot it hovering in front of flowers like hummingbirds do, sucking up nectar with its giant **proboscis**, or feeding tube. **This hungry, hovering bug has superpowered vision to help it find the nectar.**

Fast food

Hovering uses lots of energy, so the hawk-moth needs to feed in the **shortest time possible**. Guided by **ultraviolet patterns** on flowers, the moth **angles its proboscis** to exactly the right spot. That's like you trying to put a straw that's as long as you are into a glass with just your mouth! Using vision to **precisely move the body** is common in mammals, but it's **extremely rare** in insects.

The moth's compound eyes are so sensitive that they can detect UV patterns with just one ommatidium.

The hummingbird hawk-moth's proboscis is nearly as long as its body. It's curled up when not in use.

The long hairs on the hummingbird hawk-moth's body look like the feathers and tail of a real hummingbird.

Eye View Checklist

- See in the dark
- See underwater
- See in very bright light ✔
- See all around them ✔
- Focus on something in the distance
- Focus on something up close ✔
- Good at detecting movement

A hummingbird's wings beat about 50 times per second, while the hawk-moth's move at an impressive 80 beats per second, helping it stay still in the air.

Constant color

Many hawk-moth species are active at **dawn and dusk**—the times when light levels change fastest—so they need to be able to find their **favorite flowers** in different conditions. Using experiments based on food rewards, scientists discovered that hawk-moths could **still tell colors apart** even when the light was **100 times dimmer** or even a different color.

Dial it up

Like many moths, the hummingbird hawk-moth's close cousin, the **elephant hawk-moth**, is active at night. Unlike the others, this moth can **still see colors**, even in the darkest hours. As the stars come out, the elephant hawk-moth "turns up the dial" on its vision to boost the images on its retinas. It **tunes out** the things it doesn't need to see and **slows its vision down**—all without the world becoming too blurry.

Now turn the page for an imaginary view of what the hummingbird hawk-moth sees when it's looking for nectar . . .

Our eye view

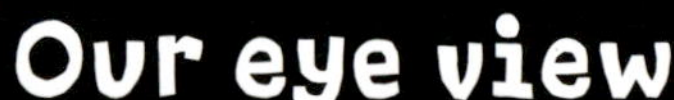

A hummingbird hawk-moth is out flying, looking for its last feed of the day . . .

Its favorite flowers are swaying in the breeze. Will it be able to wield its huge proboscis and get to the nectar?

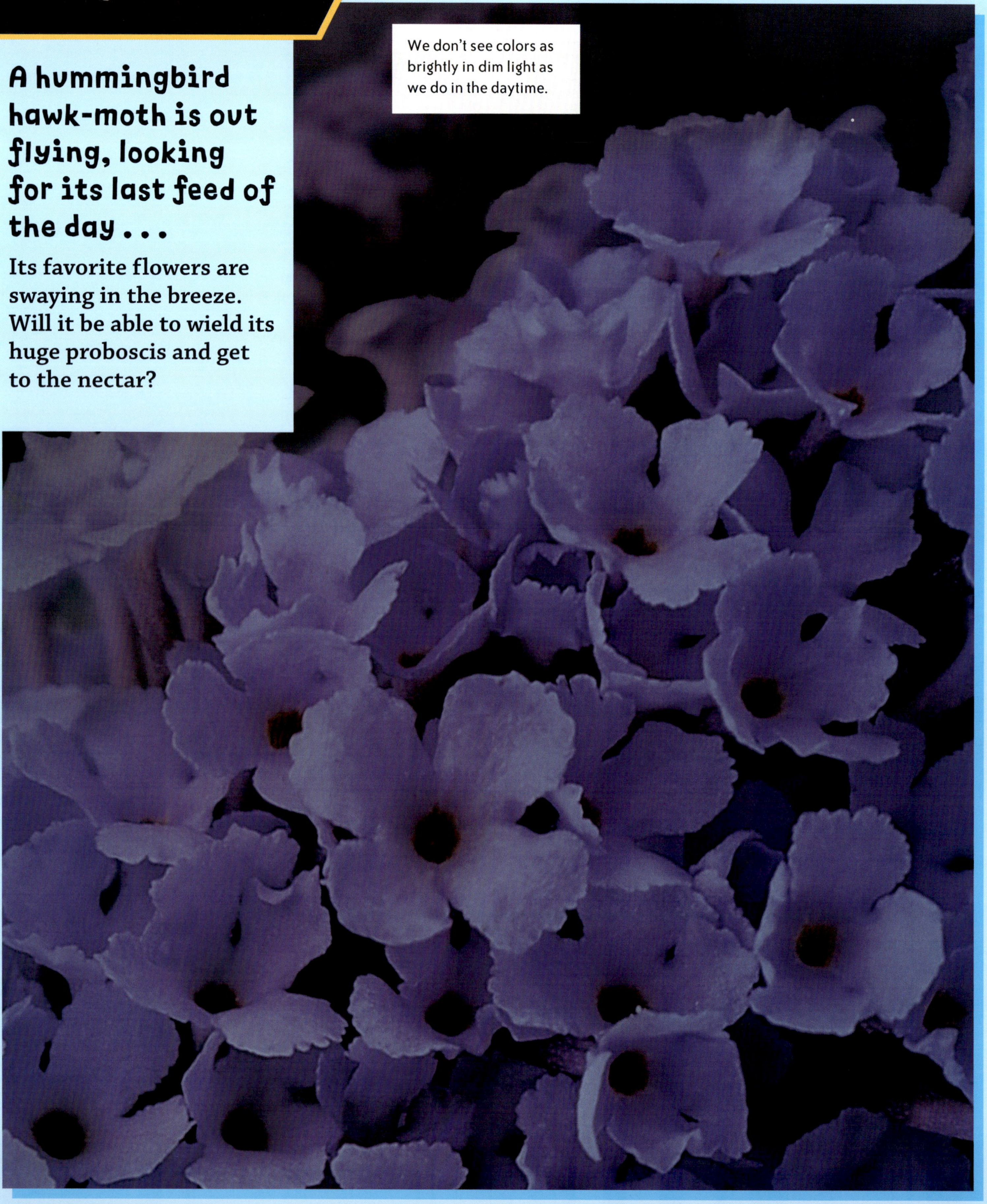

We don't see colors as brightly in dim light as we do in the daytime.

A hummingbird hawk-moth's eye view!

Horse fly

This bug looks like it's wearing
wacky wraparound shades, but
these stylish eyes are NOT for fashion.
They are searching for a bite to eat!

Bloodthirsty fly

The horse fly gets its name because it bites horses, but this critter is not fussy—cows, deer, humans, and other large mammals are all on its list of victims. A male horse fly feeds only on nectar, but the female needs a protein-packed meal of blood in order to make eggs. **She is on a gruesome mission to drink fresh blood.**

Eye View Checklist

- See in the dark
- See underwater
- See in very bright light ✔
- See all around them ✔
- Focus on something in the distance
- Focus on something up close
- Good at detecting movement ✔

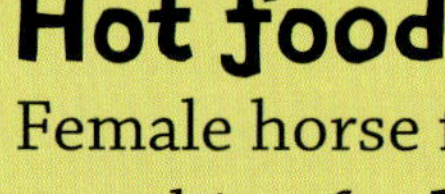

Hot food

Female horse flies find food by searching for **large, moving shapes** that stand out against the green grass. They have special **heat-detecting vision** that helps them pick out their warm-blooded prey. **Dark fur** absorbs more of the sun's heat, making black animals especially eye-catching to hungry horse flies!

A black coat absorbs more heat than a paler one.

A special camera shows that the top of the animal is warmer than the rest because it faces the sun.

The markings on the horse fly's compound eyes are created by pigments in the tiny hexagonal facets. Scientists don't know why the flies have these crazy patterns.

A horse fly can smell your breath! Its antennae detect carbon dioxide—the gas that all animals breathe out.

Studies show that **checks** and **stripes dazzle** horse flies, which prevents them from landing and biting. **Zebra-print coats** are sometimes used as a protective cover for horses!

Super stunts

All flies have **super-fast reactions**, making them very hard to swat, but female horse flies are determined feeders as well as nimble fliers. They perform amazing **mid-air flips** so that they can quickly return for another attempt at landing on their victim.

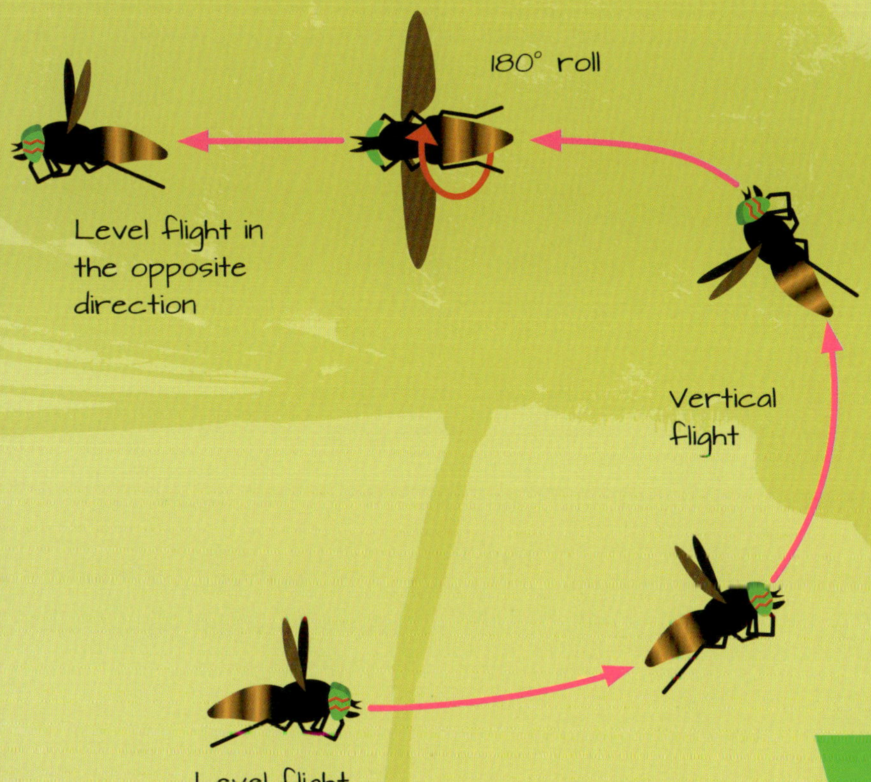

Love spots

You can tell a harmless male from a bloodsucking female by the size of his eyes. A **male's eyes** are **larger** than the female's, to give him the best chance of finding a mate. Not only that, but his eyes have a **special forward-facing area** designed to detect the movement of small objects. This helps him to **spot and follow** fast-flying females.

The male's big field of vision is useful for spotting small objects, like a female horse fly.

A female can make do with a smaller field of vision because she is looking for large mammals.

Now turn the page for an imaginary view of what the horse fly sees when it's in a meadow...

Our eye view

We can see shapes and details clearly, but our eyes are not able to detect heat.

It's a warm, sunny day, and a female horse fly is waiting in the long grass for her prey to pass by . . .

She has located an easy victim that can't swat her away, but she needs to be fast—the sky is full of other awesome aviators today.

Swallows swoop across the meadow, snapping up horse flies and other insects in mid-air.

The zigzag coat dazzles the horse fly, so it looks for an easier target.

A horse fly's eye view!

Glossary

360-degree vision—the ability to see all around in a full circle

binocular vision—an overlapping **field of vision** from two eyes

camera eye—a type of eye that has a **lens** and a **retina**

canthus—in dung beetles, a ridge that divides the upper and lower parts of the eye

compound eye—a type of eye that has hundreds or thousands of **facets**. Under each facet is an **ommatidium**.

cone—a type of **photoreceptor** that can detect colors in bright light

eye spot—a marking on an animal's body that looks like the big eye of another, larger creature. Eye spots are usually used to trick a predator into thinking its prey is more dangerous than it really is.

facet—one face of a many-sided object. The curved surface of a **compound eye** is made up of hundreds or thousands of facets.

field of vision—the area that is visible when the eyes are fixed in one position

focus—seeing sharp, clear images

fovea—a part of the **retina** that is packed with **photoreceptors**. This area gives clearer vision than the rest of the retina.

hexagon—a six-sided object. **Compound eyes** have hexagonal **facets**.

infrared—a part of the light **spectrum** with a longer **wavelength** than humans can see. Some animals can see infrared.

lens—a part of the eye that focuses, or directs, light on to the **retina** to give clear vision. *See also* **focus**.

Milky Way—the huge collection of stars, gas, and dust that forms our galaxy

monochrome—shades of a single color. It is often used when referring to black, white, and shades of gray.

ocelli—**simple eyes** that have a lens but no retina. They can sense light and movement. One simple eye is an ocellus.

ommatidium—a cone-shaped section under the **facets** of a **compound eye**. Each of the thousands of ommatidium in an animal's eye contains a **lens** and **photoreceptors**.

peripheral vision—what can be seen at the edges of the **field of vision** without turning the head or moving the eyes

photoreceptor—a cell that turns light into signals that can be understood by the brain

pigment—a natural color in animals or plants

pinhole eyes—**simple eyes** that have a tiny opening to let in a small amount of light

pixel—a small part of a larger image

predator—an animal that hunts other animals to eat

prey—an animal that is hunted by other animals for food

pseudopupil—the part of a **compound eye** that is directly facing an object. It looks like a black dot, or **pupil**, because all the light entering the eye is absorbed, with nothing reflected back out.

pupil—the black hole at the center of the eye. It gets larger and smaller to let in different amounts of light.

retina—the layer at the back of the eye that receives light and sends information to the brain as a signal. *See also* **fovea**.

rod—a type of **photoreceptor** responsible for vision in dim light

simple eye—a cluster of **photoreceptors** that can sense light but cannot form images. *See also* **ocelli**.

spectrum—the colors that a beam of light can be separated into: red, orange, yellow, green, blue, indigo, and violet. **Ultraviolet** and **infrared** are the parts of the light spectrum that humans cannot see.

stereopsis—how the brain combines the views from each eye to create a single, three-dimensional image. *See also* **binocular vision**.

ultraviolet (UV)—light at the far end of the **spectrum** with a shorter **wavelength** than humans can see. Many insects and birds can see ultraviolet light.

wavelength—the distance between two peaks of light waves. Each color of the **spectrum** travels in waves of different lengths. **Infrared** has the longest wavelength and **ultraviolet** has the shortest.

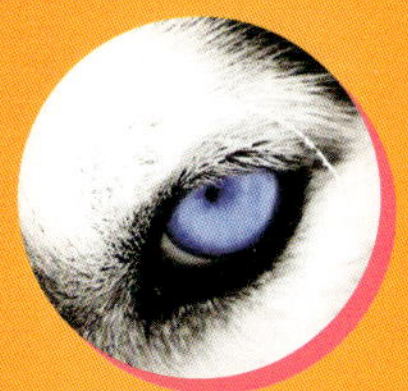

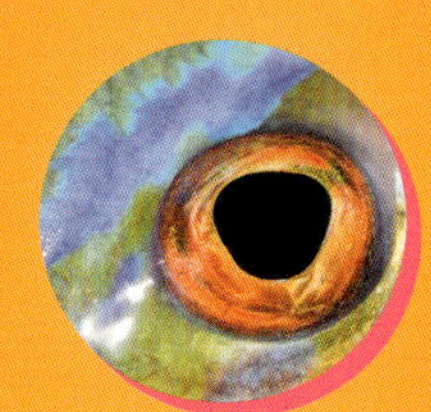

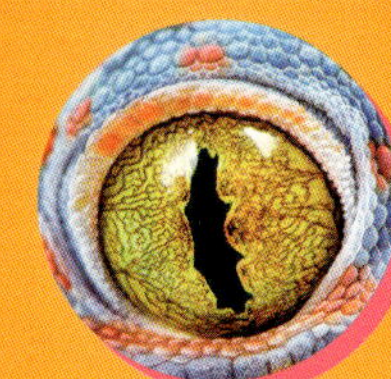

weldon**owen**

Published by Weldon Owen Children's Books
An imprint of Weldon Owen International, L.P.
A subsidiary of Insight Editions
PO Box 3088
San Rafael, CA 94912
www.insighteditions.com

Produced by iSeek Ltd.
1A Stairbridge Court, Bolney Grange Business Park,
Haywards Heath, RH17 5PA, UK
12 Hatch Street Lower, Dublin D02 R682, Ireland

INSIGHT EDITIONS
CEO: Raoul Goff
SENIOR PRODUCTION MANAGER: Greg Steffen

WRITTEN BY Catherine Ard
ILLUSTRATED BY Mat Edwards
CONSULTANT: Professor Nicholas Roberts, University of Bristol
SENIOR EDITOR: Pauline Savage
SENIOR DESIGNER: Clive Savage
MANAGING EDITOR: Toni Stemp
CREATIVE DIRECTOR: Tony Potter

ISBN: 979-8-88674-253-4

Manufactured in China by Insight Editions.
First printing, November 2025. DRM1125

10 9 8 7 6 5 4 3 2 1

Insight Editions, in association with Roots of Peace, will plant two trees for each tree used in the manufacturing of this book.

PICTURE CREDITS:
All Shutterstock, except:
p.2–3 iStock, Michael Zeigler; p.6 (bottom right) iStock, ifish; p.24 iStock, NNehring; p.25 (top) Nature Picture Library, TOM MANGELSON (bottom) iStock, Michael Zeigler; p.37 (top) Blue Planet Archive/WaterFrame/ Daniela Dirscherl; p.43 Alamy, WILDLIFE GmbH; p.48 (right) iStock, Utopia_88; p.54 (right) Alamy, David Fleetham; p.55 (bottom left) iStock, ifish.